Annie Apple is in an apple tree.

Tick the boxes as you find each thing in the big picture.

 apple

 arrow

 ant

Annie Apple's Action Trick: bite into an imaginary apple.

Bouncy **B**en can see a **b**ig, **b**lue **b**utterfly.

Tick the boxes as you find each thing in the big picture.

butterfly

bird

ball

Bouncy Ben's Action Trick: shoot your arms up for ears and wiggle them.

Clever Cat's cake has candles on it. Can you count them?

Tick the boxes as you find each thing in the big picture.

cake

candles

clock

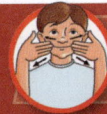
Clever Cat's Action Trick: stroke imaginary whiskers across your cheeks.

Dippy Duck is drawing a dog.

Tick the boxes as you find each thing in the big picture.

dog

dinosaur

drum

Dippy Duck's Action Trick: Flap your elbows like a waddling duck.

Eddy Elephant can catch every egg!

Tick the boxes as you find each thing in the big picture.

egg

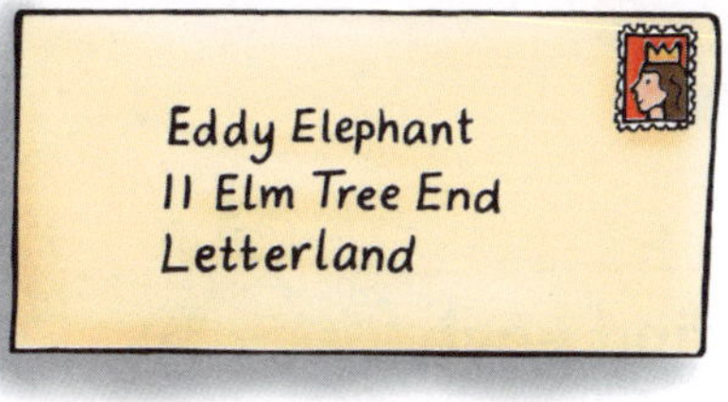

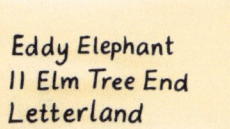
envelope

 **Eddy Elephant's Action Trick:** spread your hands out by your ears and flap them like an elephant.

5

Firefighter Fred is feeding five fish.

Tick the boxes as you find each thing in the big picture.

  fish   flower  frog

 **Firefighter Fred's Action Trick:** hold and point an imaginary hose towards an imaginary fire.

Golden Girl has a very greedy goat!

Tick the boxes as you find each thing in the big picture.

  goat ☐    grapes ☐    glasses ☐

 **Golden Girl's Action Trick:** mime holding a glass of grape juice in a 'glug, glug' position.

Harry Hat Man has a hat for his horse.

Tick the boxes as you find each thing in the big picture.

horse

hat

helicopter

Harry Hat Man's Action Trick: hold your hand in front of your mouth and breathe onto it.

Impy **I**nk can see an **i**nteresting **i**nsect.

Jumping **J**im can **j**ump as high as a **j**et.

Tick the boxes as you find each thing in the big picture.

insect   **j**et   **j**elly

 **Impy Ink's Action Trick:** touch fingers to thumb as if sticky with ink and make an 'icky' face.
Jumping Jim's Action Trick: juggle a set of imaginary balls.

9

Kicking King and his kangaroo are flying a kite.

Tick the boxes as you find each thing in the big picture.

kite

kitten

kangaroo

Kicking King's Action Trick: lift up one arm and one leg to make a K-shape.

Lucy Lamp Light likes lemons.

Tick the boxes as you find each thing in the big picture.

 lion

 leaf

 lemon

 **Lucy Lamp Light's Action Trick:** touch your fingers above your head to suggest Lucy Lamp Light's hat.

Munching Mike is munching on magnets and making a mess!

Tick the boxes as you find each thing in the big picture.

 mouse ☐

  milk ☐

  mop ☐

Munching Mike's Action Trick: rub your tummy in a circular movement.

Is Noisy Nick ten today? No, he's not, he's nine!

Tick the boxes as you find each thing in the big picture.

9 nine  nuts  nest

Noisy Nick's Action Trick: bang one fist on the other, as if hammering in a nail.

Oscar Orange is talking to an orange octopus.

Tick the boxes as you find each thing in the big picture.

 ☐

orange

 ☐

octopus

 ☐

ostrich

 **Oscar Orange's Action Trick:** form circles with your mouth and hand and look surprised.

Peter Puppy has a pretty present.

Tick the boxes as you find each thing in the big picture.

 present

 paint

 paintbrush

Peter Puppy's Action Trick: stroke down long imaginary ears.

Quarrelsome Queen is sewing her quilt quite quickly.

Tick the boxes as you find each thing in the big picture.

quilt

queen

 **Quarrelsome Queen's Action Trick:** point your finger as if asking for 'quiet!'

Red **R**obot is **r**unning to his big, **r**ed **r**ocket.

Tick the boxes as you find each thing in the big picture.

 **r**ocket ☐

 **r**abbit ☐

 **r**ainbow ☐

 **Red Robot's Action Trick:** make a running movement with your arms.

Sammy **S**nake loves **s**itting on the **s**and in the **s**un.

Tick the boxes as you find each thing in the big picture.

sun

sandcastle

starfish

Sammy Snake's Action Trick: make snake movements with your hand and arm.

Talking **T**ess loves **t**o **t**alk on her **t**elephone.

Tick the boxes as you find each thing in the big picture.

trumpet

tractor

tiger

Talking Tess's Action Trick: lift your arms horizontally to make a T-shape.

Uppy Umbrella goes up, up and away.

Tick the boxes as you find each thing in the big picture.

umbrella ☐

up ☐

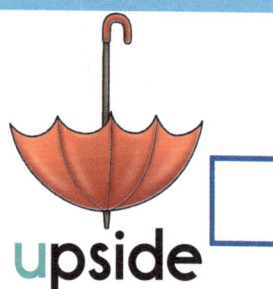
upside down ☐

Uppy Umbrella's Action Trick: hold an imaginary umbrella over your head.

Vicky Violet has some very pretty violets.

Walter **W**alrus is in the **w**ater.

Tick the boxes as you find each thing in the big picture.

violets

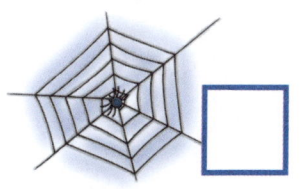
web

windmill

Vicky Violet's Action Trick: hold your hands in a V-shape.
Walter Walrus's Action Trick: flick both hands up so your arms form a W-shape.

Fix-it Max can see a fox in a box.

Tick the boxes as you find each thing in the big picture.

fox

box

six

Fix-it Max's Action Trick: cross your arms on your chest to make an X-shape.

Yellow Yo-yo Man yells, "Yellow yo-yos for sale!"

"Yellow yo-yos for sale!"

Tick the boxes as you find each thing in the big picture.

yo-yo

yellow

yacht

 **Yellow Yo-yo Man's Action Trick:** move your hands up and down as if playing with a yo-yo.

Zig Zag Zebra zooms around the zoo.

Tick the boxes as you find each thing in the big picture.

zoo

zebra

Zig Zag Zebra's Action Trick: rest your head against your hands to mime falling asleep.

Get the Letterland Action Tricks Poster at www.letterland.com and help your child take the first steps to literacy.